YIDDISH
WISDOM

To darling Cyril,

Happy birthday.

Hope you'll laugh a lot
as always.

Lots of love,
Judy

YIDDISH WISDOM

Humor and Heart
from the Old Country

ILLUSTRATIONS BY
Christopher Silas Neal

INTRODUCTION BY
Rae Meltzer

CHRONICLE BOOKS
SAN FRANCISCO

Compilation copyright © 2013 by Chronicle Books LLC.
Illustrations copyright © 2013 by Christopher Silas Neal.

Library of Congress Cataloging-in-Publication Data:

Yiddish wisdom : humor and heart from the old country / illustrations by
Christopher Silas Neal ; translation and introduction by Rae Meltzer.
    p. cm.
 In English and Yiddish (roman)
 ISBN 978-1-4521-1573-3
 1. Proverbs, Yiddish. 2. Proverbs, Yiddish—Translations into English.
I. Meltzer, Rae. II. Neal, Christopher Silas.

 PN6519.J5Y477 2013
 839'.1—dc23

Manufactured in China

MIX
Paper from
responsible sources
FSC
www.fsc.org   FSC® C104723

Design by Allison Weiner
Translation and introduction by Rae Meltzer
Special thanks to Moshe Barlev for his help.

Note on the translation and transliteration:
Translation is the process of turning or rendering one language into another.
Transliteration is the process of rendering phonetically the sound of one language
with the letters of another language. The transliterated words in this volume are
a very close approximation to the pronunciation of Yiddish words using the system
developed by the YIVO (Yiddish Scientific Institute). The acronym YIVO is a
transliteration of the first letters in the four Yiddish words that make up the name
of the organization. —R.M.

10 9 8 7 6 5 4

Chronicle Books LLC
680 Second Street
San Francisco, California 94107
www.chroniclebooks.com

From the poignant to the practical,

Yiddish proverbs have been passed along in an oral tradition for generations. In these age-old maxims there is wit, warmth, and a timeless wisdom that reflects the rich history of the Jewish people and the vibrant color of the Yiddish language.

Yiddish grew from a blend of Hebrew fragments and local German dialects in Europe's Rhine Valley a thousand years ago. As the Jews of the Rhine Valley migrated, they took Yiddish with them, which absorbed words from neighboring languages such as Russian, Polish, Czechoslovakian, Latvian, Lithuanian, and other European tongues. And just as Yiddish has roots in many languages, Yiddish words and expressions have found a home in English, through words such as *mentsh* (mature person), *maven* (expert), *shlep* (to drag), and *beygl* (bagel).

This book collects the most treasured sayings of the Yiddish language—universal, colorful, sometimes surprising—handed down to us through centuries of Jewish culture. Held in these sage words are the joys and bafflements, love and sorrow, worries and warmth, and inspiration and wonder of everyday life.

The tongue is the pen of the heart.

DI TSUNG IZ DER FEDER FUN HARTZ.

If you want to, you can move the
whole world.

AZ ME VIL, KEN MEN IBERKERN DI GANTSE VELT.

If your grandmother had a beard,
she'd be your grandfather.

VEN DI BOBBEH VOLT GEHAT A BORD,
VOLT ZI GEVEN A ZAIDEH.

Nerve succeeds!

CHUTSPEH GILT!

A little charm and you are not ordinary.

A BISSELEH CHAIN IZ SHOIN NIT GEMAIN.

From your mouth into God's ears!

FUN DEIN MOIL IN GOT'S OI'EREN AREIN!

A fault-finder complains even that
the bride is too pretty.

A CHISSOREN, DI KALLEH IZ TSU SHAIN.

An ugly patch is nicer than a pretty hole.

A MI'ESE LATE IZ SHENER VI A SHAINEH LOCH.

Teach a child in the way he should go, and
when he is old he will not depart from it.

LERNT A KIND IN DER VEG VI ER ZOL GEYN, UN
VEN ER IZ ALT VET ER NIT OPGEYN FUN DEM.

A big oven—a small loaf!

A GROISER OIVEN—A KLEINE CHALLEH!

JACK

of all trades,

MASTER

of none.

One always thinks that others are happy.

AINEM DACHT ZICH AZ BEI YENEM LACHT ZICH.

No answer is also an answer.

NIT KAIN ENTFER IZ OICH AN ENTFER.

Even in Heaven it is not good to be alone;
better to be a pair.

AFILE IN GAN-EYDN IZ OYKH NIT GUT TZU ZAYN ALEYN;
ES IZ BESER TZU ZAYN A POR.

One mother achieves more than
a hundred teachers.

EYN MAME DERGREYKHT MER VI A HUNDERT LERERS.

Everything revolves around bread and death.

ALTS DRAIT ZICH ARUM BROIT UN TOIT.

The face tells the secret.

DER PONIM ZOGT OIS DEM SOD.

LOVE is sweet,

but it's nice to have

BREAD with it.

DI LIBEH IZ ZIS, MIT BROIT IZ ZI BESSER.

Early to rise and early to wed,
no harm done.

FREE OYFSHTEYN UN FREE KHASENE HOBN, SHAT NIT.

A dream is half a prophecy.

A KHOLEM IZ A HALB NEVUE.

If the world will ever be redeemed,
it will be only through the merit of children.

OYB DI VELT VET AMOL VERN DERLAYZN,
VET ES ZAYN NOR DURKH DEM FARDINEN FUN KINDER.

Quiet streams tear away the shores.

DI SHTILEH VASSERLECH REISSEN EIN DI BREGES.

You can't ride in all directions at one time.

ME KEN NIT FOREN OIF ALLEH YARIDEN OIF AIN MOL.

The talk of the child in the street is like
the talk of his father or mother at home.

DOS VOS A KIND REDT IN GAS IZ VOS ZAYN TATE ODER
MAME REYDN IN DER HEYM.

When the heart is full, the eyes overflow.

AZ DOS HARTZ IZ FUL, GAI'EN DI OIGEN IBER.

Don't be too sweet, or they will eat you up;
don't be too bitter, or they will spit you out.

ZAY NIT TSU ZIS, ME ZOL DIKH NIT OYFESN;
ZAY NIT TSU BITER, MEN ZOL DIKH NIT OYS-SHPAYEN.

A fool falls on his back and bruises his nose.

A SHLIMAZEL FALT OIFEN RUKEN UN TSEKLAPT ZICH DI NOZ.

When a couple fights, it cools their anger.

AZ ME BEYZERT ZIKH ON GEYT OP DER KAAS.

Better the devil you know than the
devil you don't.

BESSER MITN TAIVEL VOS M'KEN EIDER MITN TAIVEL
VOS M'KEN IM NIT.

The apple doesn't fall far from the tree.

DOS EPL FALT NIT VAYT FUN BOYM.

The food is cooked

in a POT and

the PLATE

gets the honor.

SHPEIZ KOCHT MEN IN TOP UN KOVED KRIGT DER TELLER.

When you look

to the heights,

HOLD on to

your HAT.

AZ DU KUKST OIF HOICHEH ZACHEN, HALT TSU DOS HITL.

If you're going to do something wrong, enjoy it!

AZ ME EST CHAZZER, ZOL RINNEN IBER DE BORD!

Small children don't let you sleep; big children don't let you rest.

KLEYNE KINDER LOZN NIT SHLOFN; GROYSE KINDER LOZN NIT RUEN.

A wise man knows what he says; a fool says what he knows.

A KLUGER VAIST VOS ER ZOGT; A NAR ZOGT VOS ER VAIST.

God takes with one hand and gives
with the other.

GOT NEMT MIT AIN HANT UN GIT MIT DER ANDEREH.

One hand washes the other
(and both wash the face).

EIN HANT VASHT DI TSVEITEH (UN BEIDEH VASHN
DEM PONIM).

Don't rub your belly when the little fish
is still in the pond.

PATSH ZICH NIT IN BEICHELEH, VEN FISHELEH ZEINER
NOCH IN TEICHELEH.

FOOLS and WEEDS

grow without rain.

NARONIM UN KROPEVEH VAKSEN ON REGEN.

It's good to look upon a beautiful person,
but it's better to live with a smart one.

OYF A SHEYNEM PERZON IZ GUT TSU KUKN, MIT A KLUGN
IZ GUT TSU LEBN.

A meowing cat can't catch mice.

A KATZ VOS M'YAVKET KEN KAIN MEIZ NIT CHAPEN.

A frequent guest becomes a pest.

A GAST OIF A VAIL ZEIT FAR A MAYLL.

A penny at hand is worth a dollar
at a distance.

A NOENTER GROSHEN IZ BESSER VI A VEITER KERBEL.

It is hard to raise sons and much harder
to raise daughters.

ES IZ SHVER TSU HODEVEN ZIN NOR A SAKH SHVERER
TSU HODEVEN TEKHTER.

If you can't do as you wish, do as you can.

AZ ME KEN NIT VI ME VIL, TUT MEN VI ME KEN.

It's good to learn to barber on someone else's beard.

OIF A FREMDER BORD IZ GUT ZICH TSU LERNER SHEREN.

Suspense is worse than the ordeal itself.

DER'INNU-HADIN IZ ERGER VI DER DIN ALAIN.

Time brings wounds and heals them.

DI TSEIT BRENGT VUNDEN UN HAILT VUNDEN.

If you're still a child at twenty, you're an
ass at twenty-one.

AZ MEN IZ BIZ TSVANTSIK YOUR NOKH ALTS A KIND, IZ
MEN AN EYZL TSU EYN-UN-TSVANTSIK.

One link snaps, and the whole chain
falls apart.

BRECHT ZICH A RING, TSEFALT DI GANTSEH KAIT.

All of life is a struggle.

DOS GANTSEH LEBEN IZ A MILCHOMEH.

A half truth is a whole lie.

A HALBER EMES IZ AMOL A GANSTER LIGEN.

Small children, a headache; big children, a heartache.

KLEYNE KINDER, A KOPVEYTIK; GROYSE KINDER, HARTSVEYTIK.

You can't put "thank you" in your pocket.

A DANK KEN MEN IN KESHENEH NIT LEGEN.

All that glitters is not gold.

NIT ALS VOS GLANST IZ GOLD.

If you can't go

OVER,

go UNDER.

AZ ME KEN NIT ARIBER, GAIT MEN ARUNTER.

A word is like an arrow—both are in a hurry to strike.

A VORT IZ AZOI VI A FEIL—BAIDEH HOBEN GROISSEH EIL.

A heavy heart talks a lot.

A SHVER HARTZ REDT A SACH.

Trying to outsmart everybody is the greatest folly.

VELLEN ZEIN KLIGER FUN ALLEH IZ DI GRESTEH NARISHKEIT.

Man thinks and God laughs.

A MENTSH TRACHT UN GOT LACHT.

A liar must have a good memory.

A LIGNER DARF HOBEN A GUTEN ZICKORIN.

The troubles of a stranger aren't worth
an onion.

A FREMDEH TSOREH IZ KAIN TSIBELEH NI VERT.

Like soap for the body, so are tears for the soul.

VI ZEYF FARN GUF, AZOY ZAYNEN TRERN FAR DER NESHOME.

Keep on trying and you will be happy.

ME DREYT ZIKH UN ME FREYT ZIKH.

Hope for miracles but don't rely on one.

HOF OIF NISSIM NOZ FARLOZ ZICH NIT OIF A NES.

If you have money, you are wise and good-looking and can sing well too.

AZ ME HOT GELT, IZ MEN KLUG UN SHAIN UN MEN KEN GUT ZINGEN.

One old friend is better than two new ones.

AN ALTER FREINT IZ BESSER VI NEI'EH TSVAI.

When a fool goes shopping, the
storekeepers rejoice.

AZ A NAR GAIT IN MARK, FRAIEN ZICH DI KREMER.

Money buys everything except brains.

FAR GELT BAKUMT MEN ALTS, NOR NIT KAIN SAICHEL.

Words must be weighed and not counted.

VERTER MUZ MEN VEGEN UN NIT TSAILEN.

If you don't teach the ox to plow when he
is young, it will be difficult to teach
him when he is grown.

OYB DU VEST NIT LERNEN DEM OXS TSU AKERN
AZ ER IZ YUNG, VET ZAYN ZEYER SHVER IM
OYSLERNEN AZ ER IZ DERVAKSN.

In a quarrel, each side is right.

IN TOCH IZ YEDER TSAD GERECHT.

That place

seems good

WHERE

we are not.

DORTEN IZ GUT VU MIR SEINEN NITO.

It is easier to be a critic than an author.

ES IZ LAICHTER TSU ZEIN A MEVAKER VI A MECHABER.

The masses are asses.

DER OILEM IZ A GOILEM.

The pen stings worse than the arrow.

DI PEN SHIST ERGER VI A FAIL.

Another man's tidbit smells sweet.

A FREMDEH BISSEN SHMEKT ZIS.

A sleepless night is the worst punishment.

A NACHT ON SHLOF IZ DI GRESTEH SHTROF.

It is better to have nobility of character
than nobility of birth.

ES IZ BESER HOBN EYDLKAYT FUN KHARAKTER VI ZAYN
EYDL GEBORN.

LITTLE

children have

BIG EARS.

KLEINE KINDER HOBN GROISE OIREN.

That's how the cookie crumbles.

AZOY VERT DOS KIKHL TSEBROKHN.

It's easier to guard a sack of fleas than
a girl in love.

ES IZ LAICHTER TSU HITN A ZAK FLAI EIDER
A FARLIBTE MAIDEL.

Better caution at first than tears afterward.

BESSER FRI'ER BEVORENT AIDER SHPETER BEVAINT.

The smoothest way is sometimes full
of stones.

DER GLEICHSTER VEG IZ FUL MIT SHTAINER.

Joy from children is more precious
than money.

NAKHES FUN KINDER IZ MER TAYER FAR GELT.

Ask advice from everyone, but act with
your own mind.

BARAT ZICH MIT VEMEN DU VILST, UN TU MITEN
AIGENEM SAICHEL.

If you dig a pit for

SOMEONE ELSE,

you fall in it

YOURSELF.

AZ ME GRUBT A GRUB FAR YENEM, FALT MEN
ALAIN AREIN.

Dress up a

BROOM and

it will also look

NICE.

AZ MEN BATZIERT A BEZEM IZ ER OICH SHAIN.

Easy loves, heavy damages.

LEICHTEH LIBES, SHVEREH SHODENS.

There is no such thing as a bad mother.

A SHLECHTEH MAMEH IZ NITO.

Three things grow overnight:
profits, rent, and girls.

DRAY ZAKHN VAKSN IBER NAKHT: REVOKHIM,
DIREGELT, UN MEYDLAKH.

A wicked tongue is worse than an evil hand.

A BAIZEH TSUNG IZ ERGER FUN A SHLECHTER HAND.

One cross word brings on a quarrel.

FUN A VORT VERT A KWORT.

The husband is the boss—if his wife allows.

DER MAN IZ DER BALEBOS—AZ DI VEIB ZAINE LOZT.

With honey you can catch more flies
than with vinegar.

MIT HONIK KEN MEN CHAPEN MER FLIGEN VI MIT ESSIK.

All brides are beautiful; all the dead
are pious.

ALLEN KALLES ZEINEN SHAIN; ALLEH MAISSIM
ZEINEN FRUM.

Became so isn't born so.

GEVORN IZ NIT GEBORN.

When the wife is like a queen, the husband is like a king.

AZ DOS VAYB IZ A MALKE, IZ DER MAN A MEYLEKH.

Delay is good for cheese but not
for a wedding.

OPLEYGN IZ NOR GUT FOR KEZ OBER NIT
FAR A KHASENE.

Petty thieves are hanged; big thieves
are pardoned.

KLAINEH GANOVIM HENGT MEN; GROISSEH SHENKT MEN.

Everything ends in weeping.

ALTSDING LOZT ZICH OIS MIT A GEVAIN.

If you eat a bagel, only the hole remains
in your pocket.

AZ MEN EST OP DEM BAIGEL BLEIBT IN KESHENE
DER LOCH.

You can't chew with someone else's teeth.

MEN KEN NIT KAIEN MIT FREMDE TSEIN.

Husband and wife are like one flesh.

MAN UN VEIB ZEINEN AIN LEIB.

The OCEAN

cannot be emptied

with a SPOON.

ME KEN DEM YAM MIT A LEFELL NIT OIS'SHEPEN.

Not all that you know may you say.

NIT ALTS VOS DU VEYST MEGST DU ZOGN.

Laughter is heard farther than weeping.

A GELECHTER HERT MEN VEITER VI A GEVAIN.

Once parents used to teach their
children to talk; today children teach their
parents to keep quiet.

AMOL FLEGEN DI ELTERN LERNEN DI KINDER REDEN;
HEINT LERNEN DI KINDER DI ELTERN SHVEIGEN.

For the disease of stubbornness no cure exists.

FAR DEM KRONKHAYT FUN AKSHNKAYT IZ
NITO KAYN REFUE.

Experience is what we call the accumulation of our mistakes.

IBERLEBUNGEN IZ DOS VOS MEN RUFT DEM
ONKLAYBNZAM FUN UNZERE TOESN.

Easy to promise, hard to fulfill.

GRING TSU ZOGEN, SHVER TSU TROGEN.

God gives us two ears and one mouth so we can hear more and talk less.

GOT HOT GEGEBN DEM MENTSHN TSVEY OYERN UN EYN MOYL AZ DER MENTSH ZOL MER HERN UN VEYNIKER REDN.

When the father gives to his son, both laugh; but when the son gives to his father, both cry.

AZ DER TATTEH SHAINKT DEM ZUN, LACHEN BAIDEH; AZ DER ZUN SHAINKT DEM TATTEN, VAINEN BAIDEH.

He who is aware of his folly is wise.

DER VOS FARSHTAIT ZEIN NARISHKEIT IZ A KLUGER.

The heaviest burden is an empty pocket.

DER SHVERSTEH OL IZ A LAIDIKEH KESHENEH.

A man is

HANDSOME

if he is only better looking

than the DEVIL.

A MAN, AS ER IZ SHENER FUN DEM TEIVEL, IZ ER SHOIN SHAIN.

A wise man hears one word and
understands two.

A KLUGER FARSHTAIT FUN AIN VORT TSVAI.

Every ass likes to hear himself bray.

YEDER AIZEL HOT LIB TSU HERN VI ER ALEIN HIRZHET.

He who teaches a child is as if he had
created him.

DER VOS LERNT A KIND IZ AZOY VI ER HOT IM BASHAFN.

As the wallet grows, so do the needs.

VEN ES VAKST DER TEISTER, VAKSEN DI
BADERFENISHEN.

The gift is not as precious as the thought.

ES IZ NIT AZOI TEI'ER DER GESHANK VI DER GEDANK.

To seek wisdom in old age is like a mark in
the sand. To seek wisdom in youth is like
engraving on stone.

TSU ZUKHN KHOKHME IN DER ELTER IS VI A TSEYKHN IN
ZAMD. TSU ZUKHN KHOKHME IN YUGNT IZ VI GRAVYRN
OYF A SHTEYN.

Those who do not grow, grow smaller.

DI VOS VAKSN NIT, VERN KLEYNER.

Give a pig a finger and he'll want
the whole hand.

GIBB A CHAZZER A FINGER VIL ER DE GANTSEH HAND.

Better to break off an engagement than
a marriage.

BESSER DI T'NO'IM TSEREISSEN AIDER DI KETUBEH.

If one could do charity without money
and favors without aggravation,
the world would be full of saints.

TSEDOKEH ZOL KAIN GELT NIT KOSTEN UN G'MILAS-
CHASSODIM KAIN AGMAS-NEFESH NIT FARSHAFEN,
VOLTEN GEVEN IN DER VELT FIL TSADIKIM.

Rather alone than with a lowly mate.

BESSER ALAIN, AIDER GEMAIN.

Loans will get you moans.

BORGEN MACHT ZORGEN.

The world stands on three things: on money, on money, and on money.

OIF DREI ZACHEN SHTAIT DI VELT: OIF GELT, OIF GELT, UN OIF GELT.

Love me a little, but love me always.

HOB MIKH VEYNIK LIB, NOR HOB MIKH LANG LIB.

He who hesitates is lost.

VOS MER GEVART, MER GENART.

You can't sit on two horses
with one behind.

MIT EIN HINTN ZITST MEN NIT OIF TSVEI FERD.

A married daughter is like bread sliced from the loaf; she can't be reattached to her parents.

AN OYSGEGEBENE TOKHTER IZ VI AN OPGESHNITN SHTIK BROYT; ZI KEN ZIKH SHOYN MER NIT TZURIK TSUKLEPN TSU DI ELTERN.

The door to evildoing is wide, but the return gate is narrow.

AREIN IZ DI TIR BRAIT, UN AROIS IZ ZI SHMOL.

A man should ask for three things: a good wife, a good year, and a good dream.

DER MAN ZOL BETN FAR DRAY ZAKHN: A GUTE VAYB, A GUTN YOR, UN A GUTN KHOLEM.

One is greeted according to one's garb,
bidden farewell according to one's wisdom.

MEN BAGRIST NOCH DI KLEIDER, MEN BAGLEIT
NOCHEN SAICHEL.

Envy breeds hate.

FUN KIN'AH VERT SIN'AH.

Losing teeth and bearing children
ages one fast.

FARLIRN TSEYN UN HOBN KINDER VERT MEN SHNEL ALT.

What will become

of the SHEEP

if the wolf is

the JUDGE?

From the lowly potato you get the tastiest pancake.

FUN A PROSTE BULBE KUMT AROYS DI GESHMAKSTE LATKE.

You can't get ahead with keeping quiet.

DURCH SHVEIGEN KEN MEN NIT SHTEIGEN.

With a meat stew as with an engaged couple, one does not look too closely.

IN A TSHOLNT UN IN A SHIDUKH KUKT MEN NIT TSUFIL ARAYN.

He who has not tasted the bitter does
not understand the sweet.

DER VOS HOT NIT FARZUCHT BITTEREH, VAIST NIT
VOZ ZIES IZ.

Better to die upright than to live on
your knees.

BESSER TSU SHTARBEN SHTAI'ENDIK AIDER TSU
LEBEN OIF DI K'NI.

Don't put off till tomorrow what you can
do today.

LAIG NIT OP OIF MORGEN VOS DU KENST HEINT
BAZORGEN.

Blood is thicker than water.

BLUT IZ DIKER FUN VASER.

When your enemy falls, don't rejoice,
but don't pick him up either.

AZ DER SOINEH FALT, TOR MEN ZICH NIT FRAIEN,
OBER MEN HAIBT IM NIT OIF.

An imaginary illness is worse than
a real one.

AN EINREDENISH IZ ERGER VI A KRENK.

He who praises himself will be humiliated.

VER ES LIBT ZICH ALAIN, SHEMT ZICH ALAIN.

When one must, one can.

AZ ME MUZ, KEN MEN.

Better a little luck than a lot of gold.

BESER A BISL MAZL EYDER A SAKH GOLD.

For raising children you need Rothschild's
wealth and Samson's strength.

HODEVEN KINDER MUZ MEN HOBN ROTHSCHILD'S
RAYKHKAYT UN SHIMSHON'S SHTARKAYT.

Poverty hides wisdom.

DER DALES FARSHTELT DI CHOCHMA.

Where there is love and affection it is never
too crowded or lonely.

VU ES IZ LIBSHAFT UN VAREMKAYT DORT IZ KAYN MOL
ENGSHAFT ODER ELENTKAYT.

Too much modesty is half conceit.

TSU FIL ANIVES IZ A HALBER SHTOLTZ.

Silence is the fence around wisdom.

SHTILKAYT IZ DI FARTSAMUNG ARUM KHOKHME.

Husband and wife are of one body, but
they have separate pockets for their cash.

MAN UN VAYB ZAYNEN EYN LEYB OBER KESHENES
HOBN ZEY TSVEY.

If I would be like someone else, who will
be like me?

AZ ICH VEL ZEIN VI YENER, VER VET ZEIN VI ICH?

By day they're ready for divorce; by night
they're ready for bed.

BAY TOG TSUM GET; BAY NAKHT TSUM BET.

If you stay at home,
you won't wear out your shoes.

AZ MEN ZITST IN DER HAIM,
TSEREIST MEN NIT KAIN SHTIVEL.

There can never be too many drinking glasses or too many children.

KINDER UN GLEZER HOT MEN KEYN MOL NIT TSU FIL.

Still water runs deep.

SHTIL VASSER GROBT TIF.

If everybody says so, there's some truth to it.

AZ DI VELT ZOGT, DARF MEN GLOIBEN.

The most bitter misfortune can be covered
up with a smile.

DEM BITERSTEN MAZEL KEN MEN FARSHTELLEN
MIT A SHMAICHEL.

When you fight, leave the door open
for making up.

AZ DU KRIGST ZIKH, KRIG ZIKH AZOY AZ DU ZOLST
ZIKH KENEN IBERBETN.

Goodness is better than piety.

GUTSKAYT IZ BESER FUN FRUMKAYT.

The smallest vengeance poisons the soul.

DI KLENSTEH NEKOMEH FARSAMT DI NESHOMEH.

The reddest

APPLE has

a WORM

in it.

DI ROITSTEH EPEL HOT A VORM.

A mother-in-law forgets that she was once
a daughter-in-law.

DI SHVIGER FARGEST AZ ZI IZ A MOL ALEYN GEVEN
A SHNUR.

Many smiles, few wiles.

FIL SHMEICHEL, VEYNIK SAICHEL.

If you can't endure the bad, you'll not live
to witness the good.

AS MEN KEN NIT IBERHALTEN DOS SHLECHTEH, KEN MEN
DOS GUTEH NIT DERLEBEN.

Life is the greatest bargain; we get it
for nothing.

DOS LEBN IZ DI GRESTE METSIE; MEN KRIGT DOS UMZIST.

The tongue is a person's greatest enemy.

DI TSUNG IZ DEM MENTSHN'S GRESTER SOYNE.

Heaven and hell can both be had in
this world.

GANAIDEN UN GEHENEM KEN MEN BAIDEH HOBEN
OIF DER VELT.

You can't make

CHEESECAKES

out of snow.

GOMOLKES KEN MEN NIT MAKHN FUN SHNEY.

If you lie down with the dogs, you get up with the fleas.

AZ ME SHLOFT MIT HINT SHTAIT MEN OIF MIT FLAI.

When the stomach is empty, so is the brain.

AZ DER MOGEN IZ LAIDIK IZ DER MOI'ECH OICH LAIDIK.

Pray that you may never have to endure all that you can learn to bear.

MEN ZOL NIT GEPRUFT VERREN TSU VOS ME KEN GEVOINT VERREN.

The heart is small and embraces
the whole wide world.

DI KLAINER HARTZ NEMT ARUM DI GROISSEH VELT.

The highest wisdom is kindness.

DI HEKHSTE KHOKHME IZ GUT'HARTSIKAYT.

You can't dance at two weddings
at the same time.

ME KEN NIT TANTSN OYF TSVEY KHASENES
IN DER ZELBER TSAYT.

Sometimes the remedy is worse than the disease.

A MOL IZ DER REFUEH ERGER FUN DER MAKEH.